Chords

for Guitar

ERIK DARLING
TOM RIKER

SCHIRMER BOOKS
A Division of Macmillan Publishing Co., Inc.
NEW YORK

Schirmer Books
A Division of Macmillan Publishing Co., Inc.
866 Third Avenue, New York, N.Y. 10022

Library of Congress Catalog Card Number: 79-9702

Printed in the United States of America

printing number

1 2 3 4 5 6 7 8 9 10

Library of Congress Cataloging in Publication Data

Darling, Erik.
   Chords for guitar.

   1. Guitar--Chord diagrams. I. Riker, Tom
joint author. II. Title.
MT588.D33   787.6'1'0712   79-9702
ISBN 0-02-870410-X

ACKNOWLEDGMENTS

Erik Darling—One of America's great folk artists and guitar players. Erik has been a member of many groups including the Roof Top Singers (Walk Right In), The Tarriers, and the Weavers. He has written and taught for the guitar for many years.

Tom Riker—A painter and graphic designer, Tom has written and designed many books. His company Dovetail Design Works is an archive specialty house.

Photographs by Bart/LoPresti

The Bozo Guitar

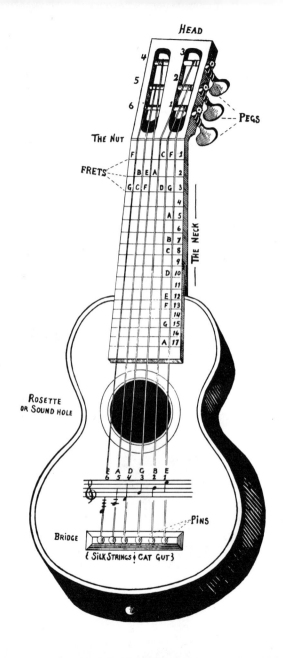

TABLE OF CONTENTS

INTRODUCTION

There are four major sections in this book.

1. Reading Chord Diagrams

2. Chords Listed Alphabetically

3. Common Blues Chords

4. Blues and Jazz Chords

Chords which are particularly useful in fingerpicking are labeled accordingly. All chords are illustrated by both photographs and diagrams.

Many of the chords can be moved up or down
the neck to get additional chords. Some particular
A chord, for example, may be able to be moved
to an A♯ or B chord, or down to an A♭ or G chord.
It works like this: Each fret on the guitar equals a
half step. Therefore, if you move a particular chord
form up the neck (toward the bridge) one fret, it is
then raised one half step, to another chord. The
half steps in music are as follows (notice there is
only a half step between B & C and E & F).

A A♯ B C C♯ D D♯ E F F♯ G G♯ A

    B♭   D♭ E♭   G♭   A♭

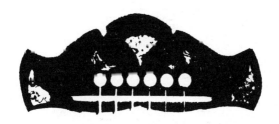

SHARPS AND FLATS

A♯ (sharp) and B♭ (flat) are different names
given to the same tone (or same chord), the
mid-point between A and B. This mid-point
is called either A-raised, A♯ sharp or B-lowered
B♭ (flat):

WITH SHARPS.

SILVER STRINGS   CATGUT STRINGS

6 5 4   3 2 1

OPEN E A D   G B E   NOTES

F	A#	D#	G#	C	F	1st Fret.
F#	B	E	A	C#	F#	2nd Fret.
G	C	F	A#	D	G	3rd Fret.
G#	C#	F#	B	D#	G#	4th Fret.
A	D	G	C	E	A	5th Fret.
A#	D#	G#	C#	F	A#	6th Fret.
B	E	A	D	F#	B	7th Fret.
C	F	A#	D#	G	C	8th Fret.
C#	F#	B	E	G#	C#	9th Fret.
D	G	C	F	A	D	10th Fret.
D#	G#	C#	F#	A#	D#	11th Fret.
E	A	D	G	B	E	12th Fret.

8

WITH FLATS.

SILVER STRINGS   CATGUT STRINGS

6 5 4   3 2 1

OPEN   NOTES

F	Bb	Eb	Ab	C	F	1st Fret.
Gb	B	E	A	Db	Gb	2nd Fret.
G	C	F	Bb	D	G	3rd Fret.
Ab	Db	Gb	B	Eb	Ab	4th Fret.
A	D	G	C	E	A	5th Fret.
Bb	Eb	Ab	Db	F	Bb	6th Fret.
B	E	A	D	Gb	B	7th Fret.
C	F	Bb	Eb	G	C	8th Fret.
Db	Gb	B	E	Ab	Db	9th Fret.
D	G	C	F	A	D	10th Fret.
Eb	Ab	Db	Gb	Bb	Eb	11th Fret.
E	A	D	G	B	E	12th Fret.

9

MOVING CHORDS

If you move an A chord one fret up (a half step),
it becomes an A♯ (or B♭) chord. If you move it
up another fret (two frets in all), it becomes a B
chord. If you move the B chord up one fret
(a half step), it becomes a C chord—there is only a
half step between B & C.

An important rule to remember, when moving
some particular chord, is that you may only
be able to play the <u>fretted strings</u>. If you were
to move the A chord, the first one in this
book, up two frets, to a B position, and strummed
all six strings— three fretted and three open— it
would sound terrible, if a B chord is what you
wanted to hear. This accounts for the need to
bar unfretted strings sometimes. The first B
chord in this book represents an A chord moved
up to a B position and barred:

A─────to───B position

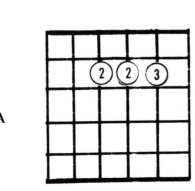

A

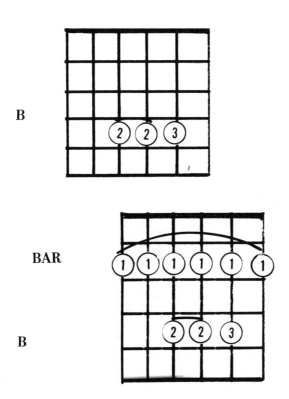

B

BAR

B

The chord which may sound terrible, however, when moved up the neck, when you have one thing in mind, may sound great with another thing in mind, in a different context. There are no rules that must be followed. It becomes a matter of what sounds right.

The alphabetical listing of chords starts with the A chords, is followed by the Am (minor) chords, then the A# chords, then the B chords, and so on.

The next section of this book, Reading Chord Diagrams, will explain how the diagram-symbols work, and, as well, the basic hand and finger positions necessary to form chords easily.

Steal way to it freely. Have it be a passion, a privacy, an expression of values. It can be a time of sanity no matter what else is going on.

CORRECT POSITION

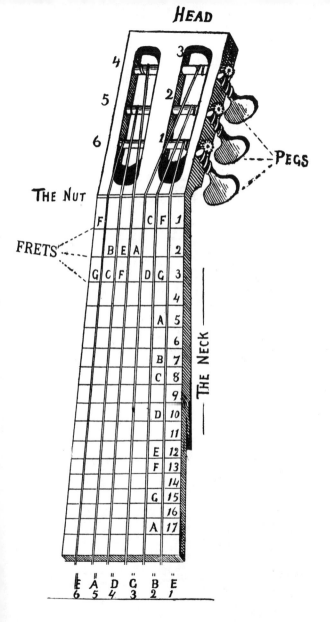

HEAD

4

3

5

2

6

1

PEGS

THE NUT

F   C F | 1

FRETS

B E A | 2

G C F   D G | 3

| 4

A | 5

| 6

B | 7

C | 8

| 9

D | 10

THE NECK

| 11

E | 12

F | 13

| 14

G | 15

| 16

A | 17

E A D G B E
6 5 4 3 2 1

13

The following drawing may not end up in the permanent collection of the Museum of Modern Art, but it will demonstrate what finger is indicated on the charts

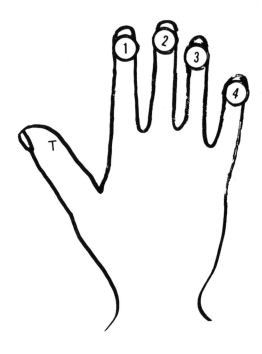

READING CHORD DIAGRAMS AND MAKING CHORDS

The same finger indicated on two strings and connected by a curved line signifies that you fret the two strings by partially barring.

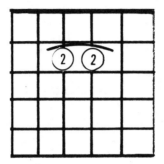

If there is no curved line. you use the end of your finger placed carefully between the two strings, and very close to the fret:

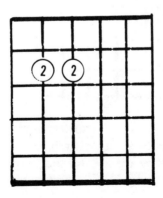

All six strings fretted signifies a full bar:

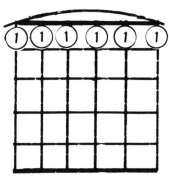

An X <u>at the end of a string</u> signifies that the string is not part of that chord, and therefore, should not be played. An X <u>on a string</u> signifies that the string is muted, usually by an adjacent finger. In this case, it would be the third.

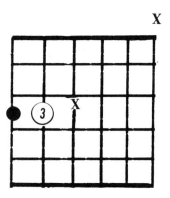

A solid dot means that you fret the dotted string (at the dot) with an adjacent finger <u>when you play it.</u> In this case, it would be the sixth string, third fret, with the third finger.

MAKING CHORDS

The <u>basic open chord position</u> has the thumb
around the neck, the palm out, and the edge
of your hand snug to the back of the neck:

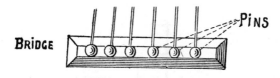

BRIDGE   PINS

The basic bar chord position has the thumb in the
back of the neck, the first finger as straight as
possible, and fretting all six strings:

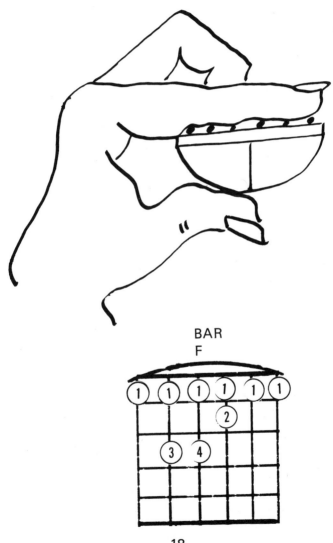

BAR
F

The half finger bar position has the first finger
bent and barring only three or four strings:

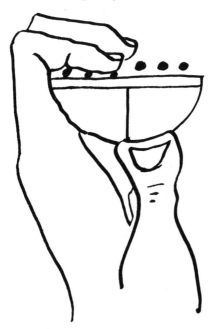

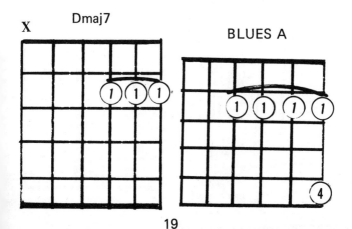

The thumb chord position has the whole palm
snug to the neck, the thumb around, over the
top edge of the fingerboard and fretting the
sixth string.

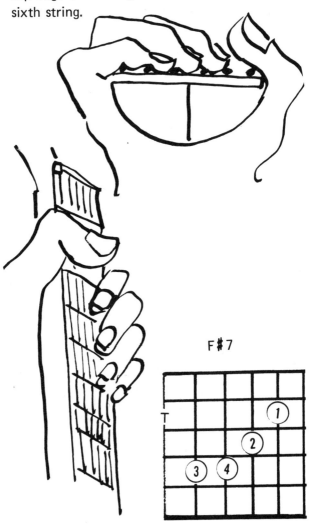

F#7

FINGERS

Arched and fretting a single string:

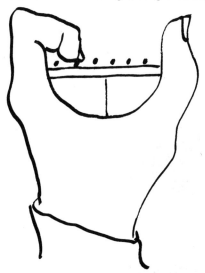

F

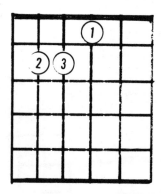

<u>Buckled inward</u>, partially barring two or three strings:

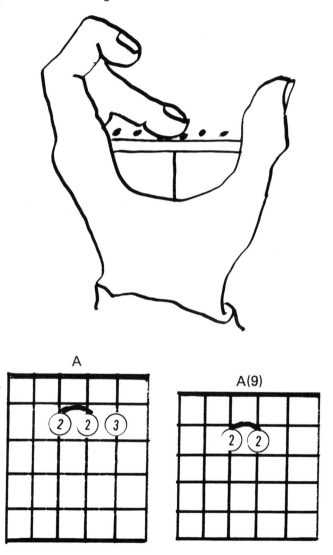

A

A(9)

Fretting a string, and muting adjacent strings:

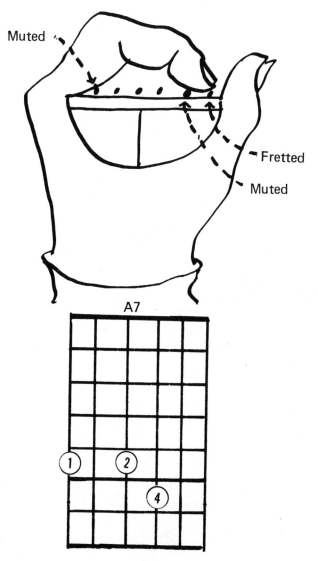

Muted

Muted

Fretted

A7

ALPHABETICAL

A
Am

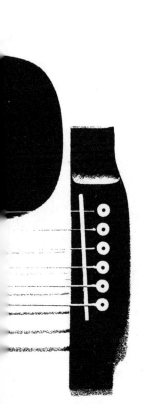

A#
Bb

LISTING OF CHORDS

A

A7

A7(sus4)

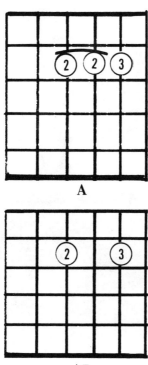

A

A7

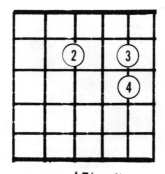

A7(sus4)

A9

A(9)

A6

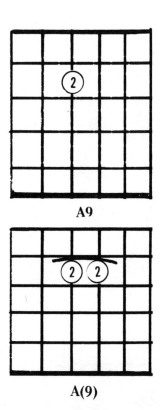

A9

A(9)

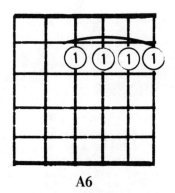

A6

29

A(sus4)

Bar A

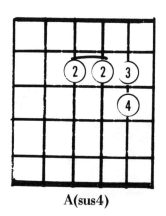

A(sus4)

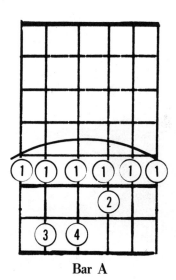

Bar A

A7

Adim7

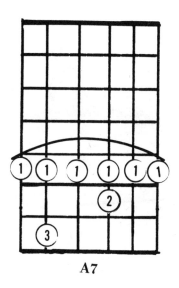

A7

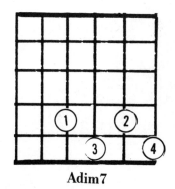

Adim7

Amaj7

Amaj7

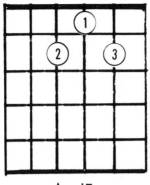

Amaj7

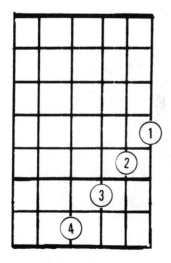

Amaj7

Amaj7

Church Bells A

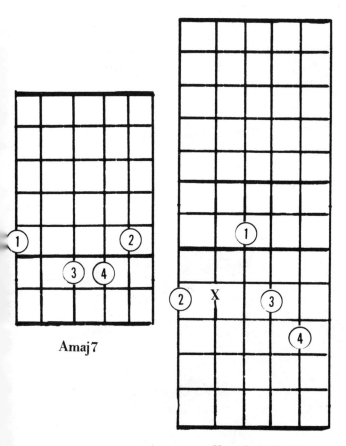

Amaj7

Church Bells A

Fingerpicking

A9

A7

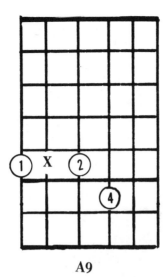

A9

Fingerpicking

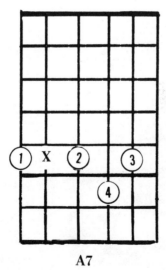

A7

Am

Am7

Am7

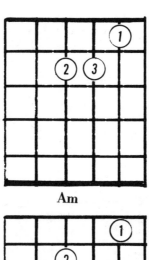

Am

Am7

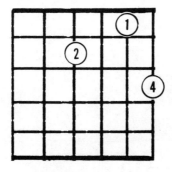

Am7

Am6

Am7

Am

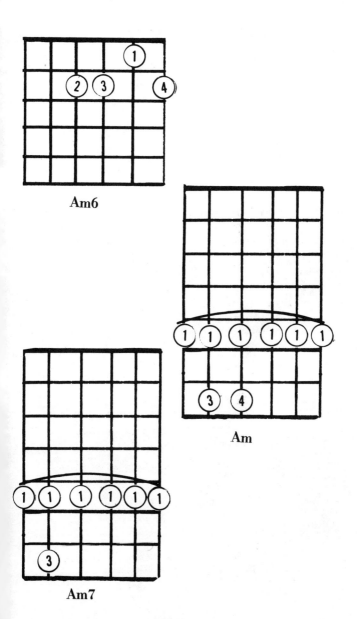

Am6

Am

Am7

Am7

Am

Am

44

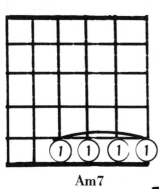

Am7

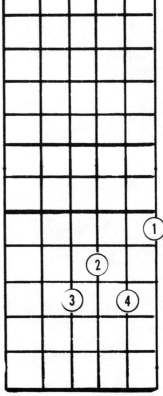

Am

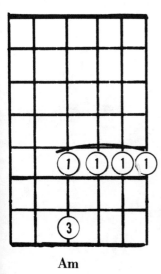

Am

A♯ B♭

A♯7 B♭7

A♯ maj7 B♭ maj7

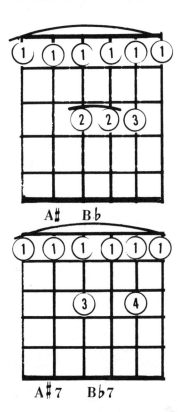

A♯   B♭

A♯7   B♭7

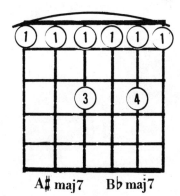

A♯ maj7   B♭ maj7

A♯   B♭

A♯7   B♭7

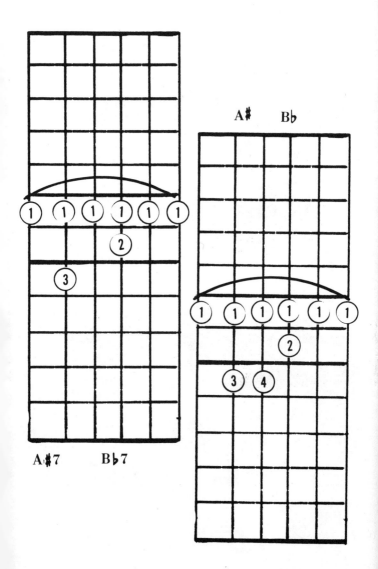

A♯   B♭

A♯7   B♭7

49

A♯ maj7   B♭ maj7

A♯ 7   B♭ 7

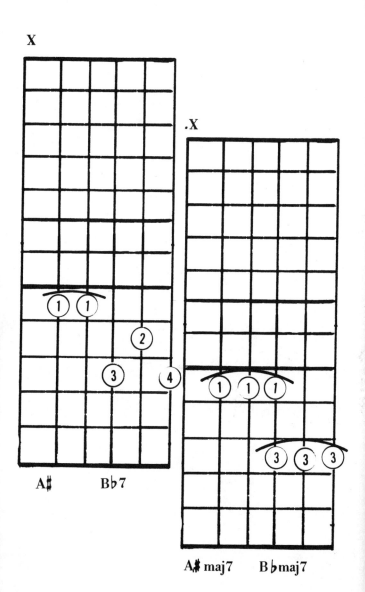

X

.X

A♯   B♭7

A♯maj7   B♭maj7

51

A♯m   B♭m

A♯ 7   B♭ 7

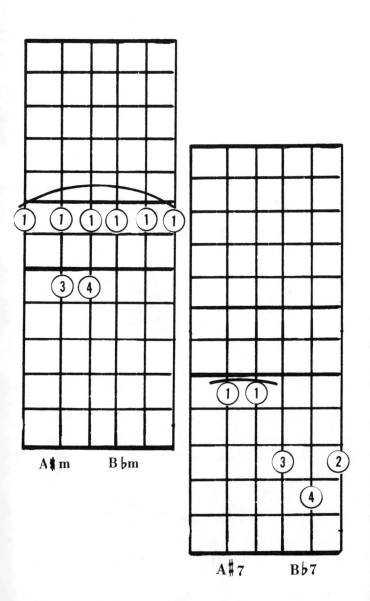

A♯m   B♭m

A♯7   B♭7

A♯9

A♯m   B♭m

A♯m7   B♭m7

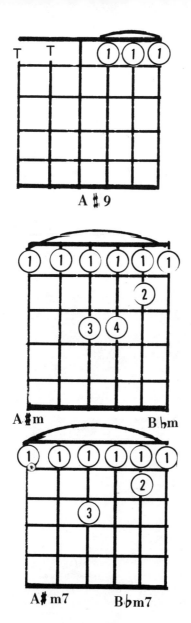

A♯9

A♯m   B♭m

A♯m7   B♭m7

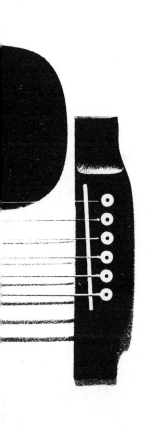

B
Bm

B

That Old B7

B7

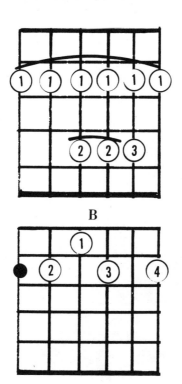

B

That Old B7

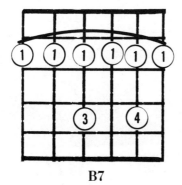

B7

B6

Bmaj7

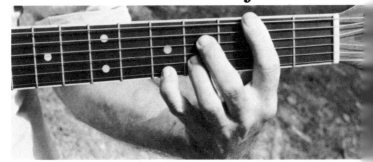

B7

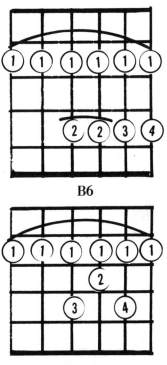

B6

Bmaj7

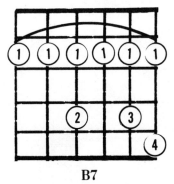

B7

B6

B7

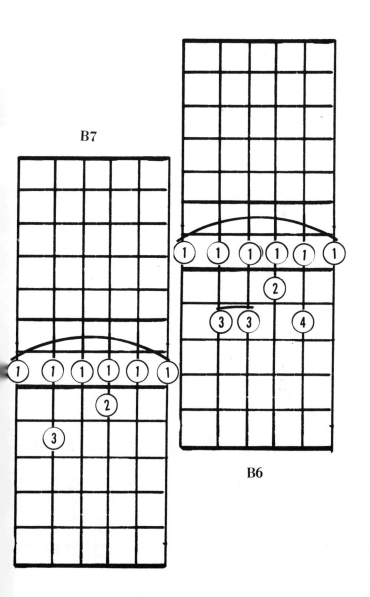

B7

B6

Bdim7

B7

Full B7

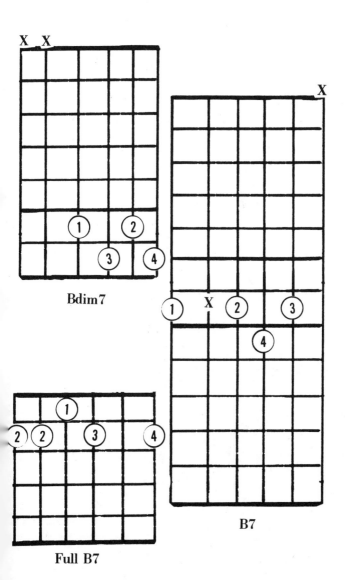

Bdim7

Full B7

B7

65

B

B

B

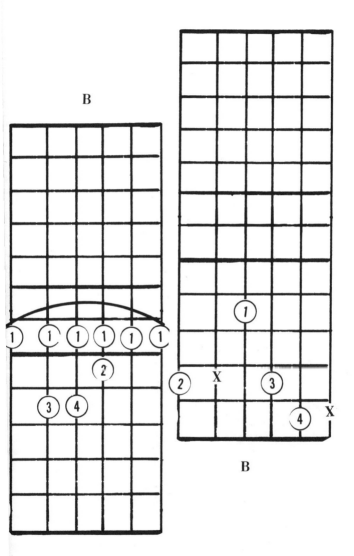

B

Bm

Bm7

Bm7

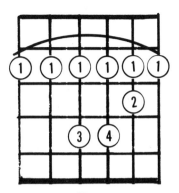

Bm

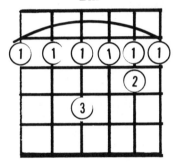

Bm7

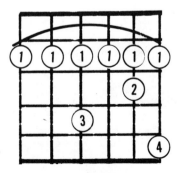

Bm7

Bm

Bm7

Bm7

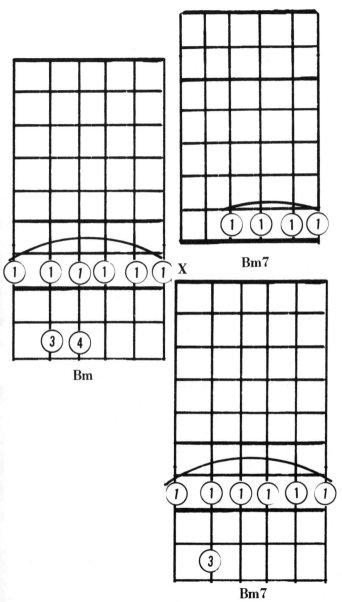

Bm

Bm7

Bm7

C
Cm

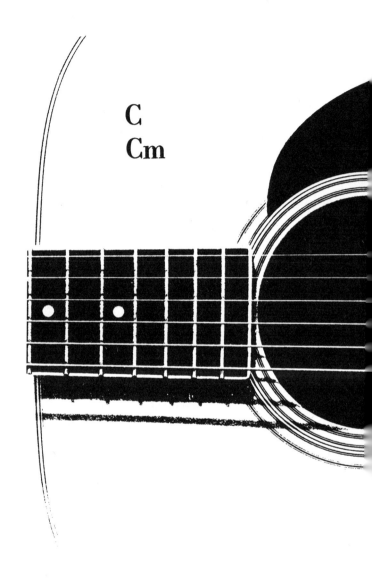

C#
Db

Full C

C

C7

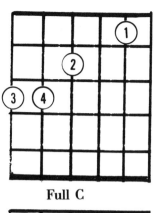

Full C

C

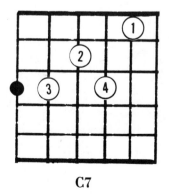

C7

C (E bass)

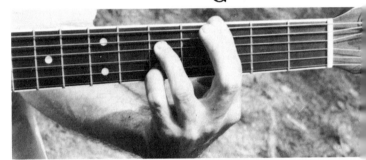

C

C7

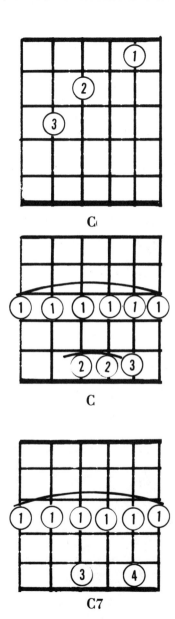

C

C

C7

C7

C7

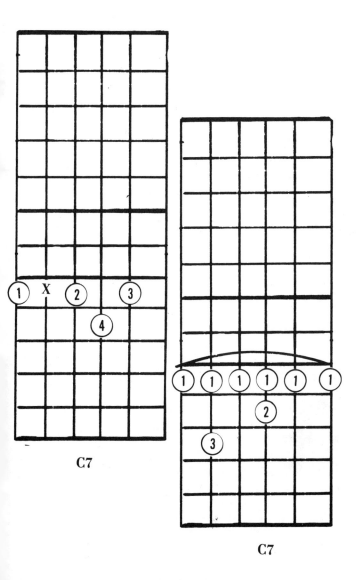

C7

C7

C6

C

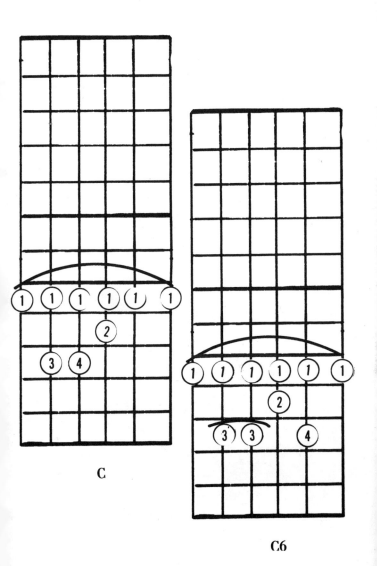

C

C6

FINGERPICKING

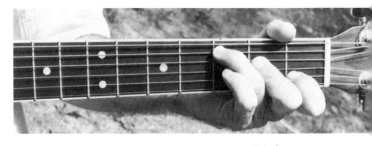

C6

C(treble G)

C(9)

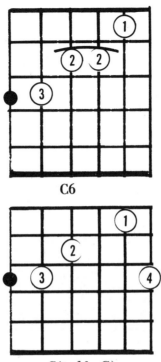

C6

C(treble G)

FINGERPICKING

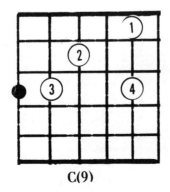

C(9)

Fingerpicking

C9

Cmaj7

Cmaj7

84

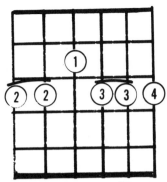

Fingerpicking   C9

Cmaj7

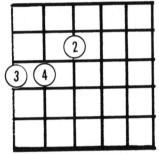

Cmaj7

Cm

Cm7

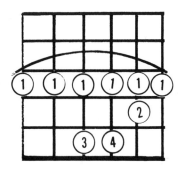

Cm

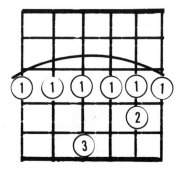

Cm7

Cm7

Cm7

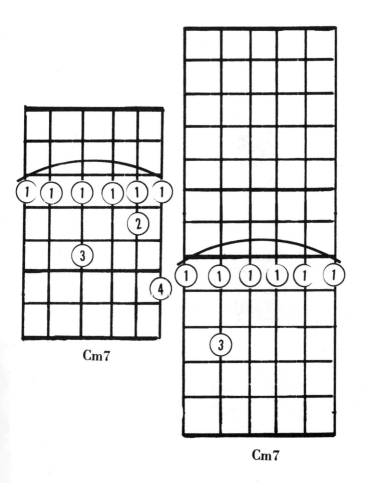

Cm7

Cm7

Cm

Cm

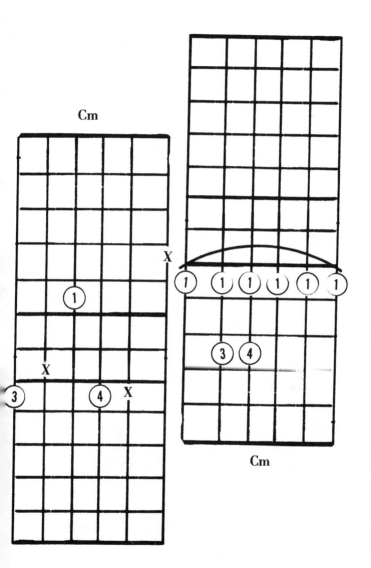

Cm

Cm

C♯ (F bass)   D♭ (F bass)

C♯   D♭

C♯7   D♭7

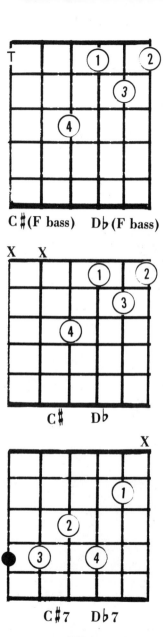

C♯(F bass)　　D♭(F bass)

C♯　　D♭

C♯7　　D♭7

93

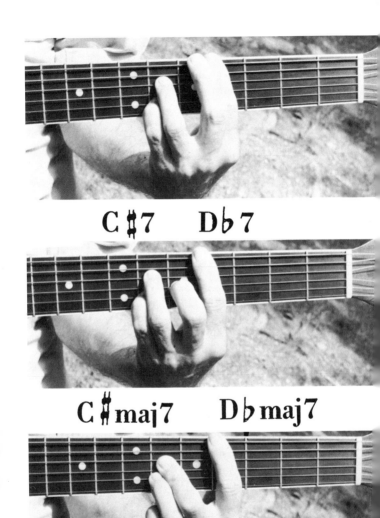

C♯7   D♭7

C♯maj7   D♭maj7

C♯   D♭

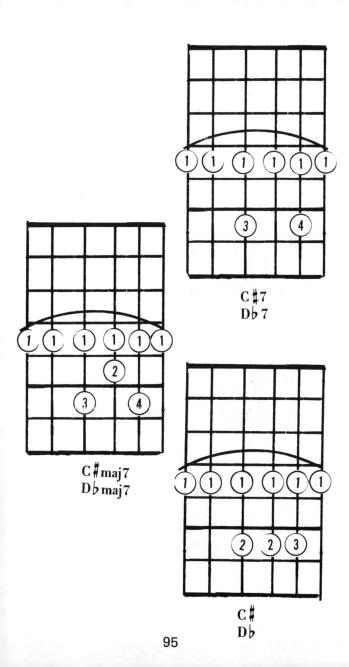

C♯7
D♭7

C♯maj7
D♭maj7

C♯
D♭

C♯dim7   D♭dim7

C♯m   D♭m

C♯m   D♭m

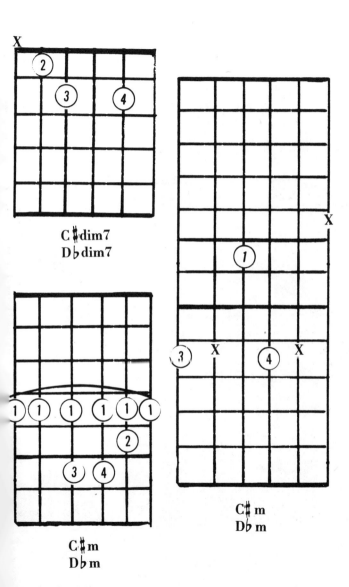

C♯dim7
D♭dim7

C♯m
D♭m

C♯m
D♭m

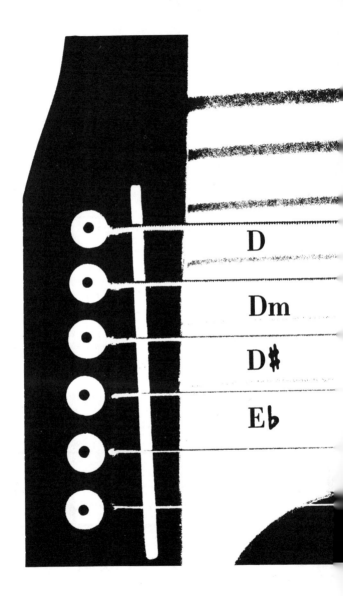

D

Dm

D#

Eb

D

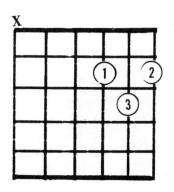

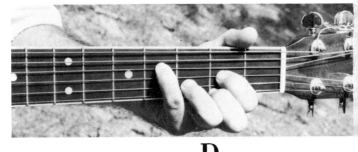

D

D7

D6

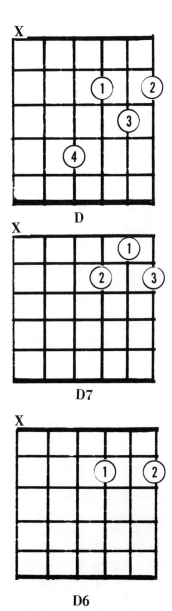

D

D7

D6

D(sus4)

D (F♯ bass)

D (F♯ bass)

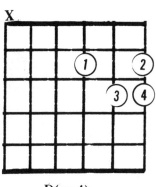

D(sus4)

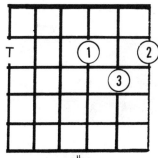

D (F#bass)

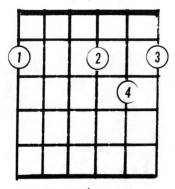

D (F#bass)

103

Dmaj7

Ddim7

Dmaj7

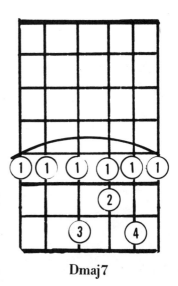

Dmaj7

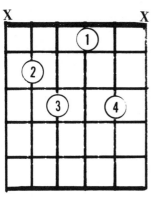

Ddim7

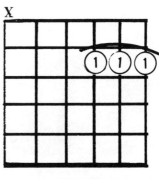

Dmaj7

FINGERPICKING

D9

Old Jazz D9

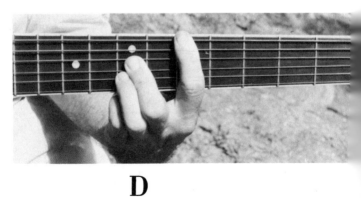

D

FINGERPICKING

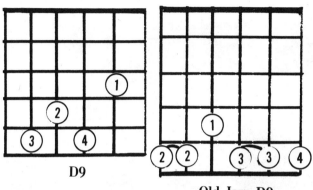

D9

Old Jazz D9

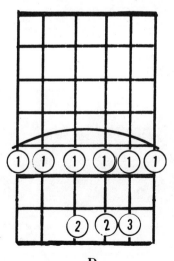

D

CHORDS IN D–TUNING
(Low E down to D)

D

G6

A

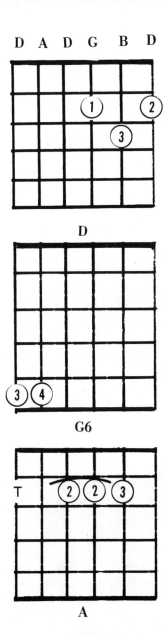

D A D G B D

D

G6

A

Dm

Dm (F bass)

Dm7

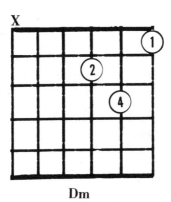

Dm

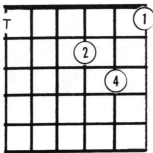

Dm (F bass)

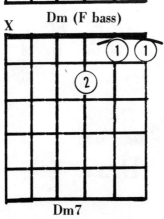

Dm7

Dm

Dm6

Dm7

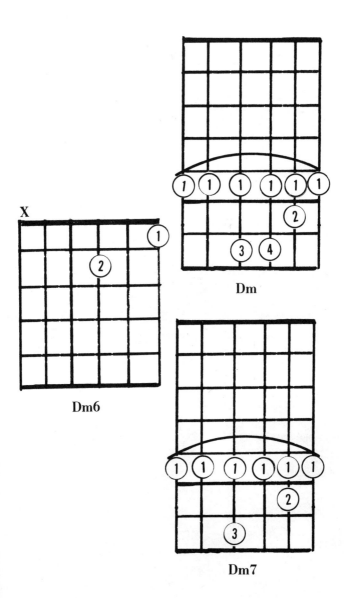

Dm6

Dm

Dm7

IN D–TUNING
(Low E down to D)

Dm

A7

Gm

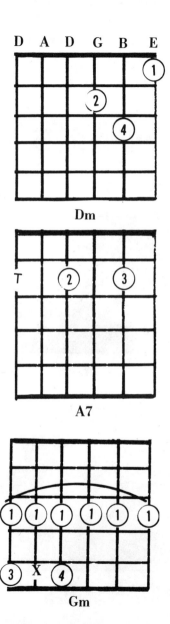

Dm

A7

Gm

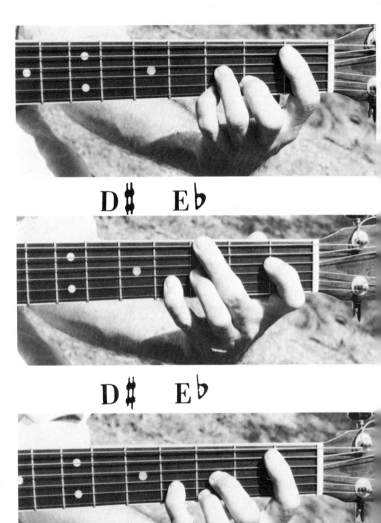

D♯   E♭

D♯   E♭

D♯7   E♭7

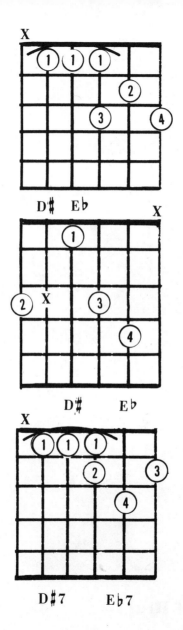

D♯   E♭

D♯   E♭

D♯7   E♭7

D♯7 E♭7

D♯7 E♭7

D♯maj7 E♭maj7

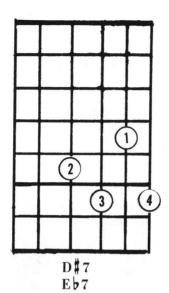

D#7
Eb7

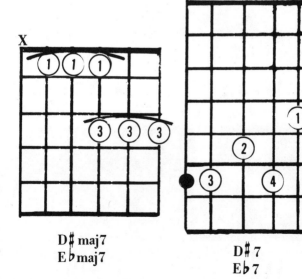

D#maj7
Ebmaj7

D#7
Eb7

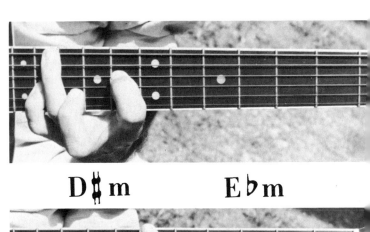

D♯m   E♭m

D♯m   E♭m

D♯m7   E♭m7

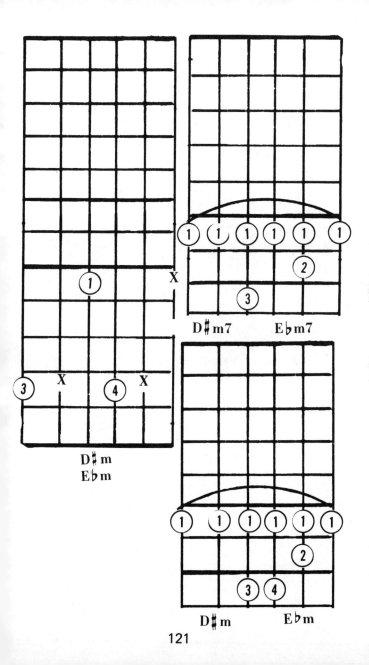

D♯m
E♭m

D♯m7   E♭m7

D♯m   E♭m

121

E

Em

E

Open E7

Old E7

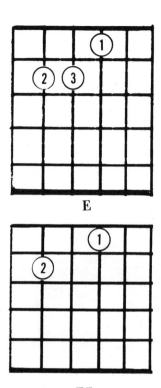

E

Open E7

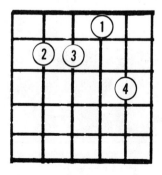

Old E7

E6

E(sus4)

Edim7

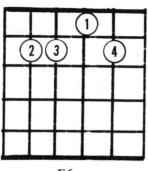

E6

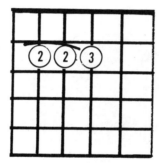

E(sus4)

X

Edim7

127

E

E

E (D-form)

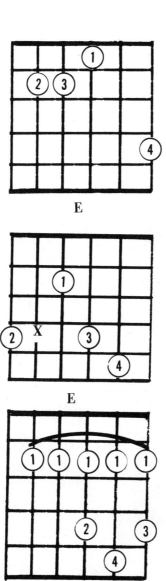

E

E

E (D-form)

E7 (C-form)

Emaj7

E7

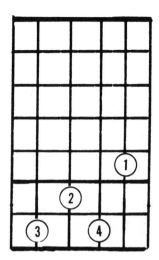

E7 (C-form)

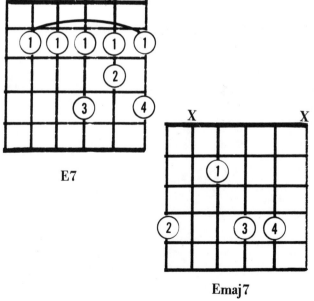

E7

Emaj7

E7

Emaj7

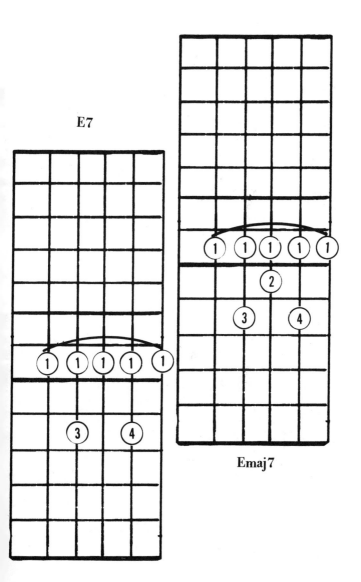

E7

Emaj7

E9

Emaj7

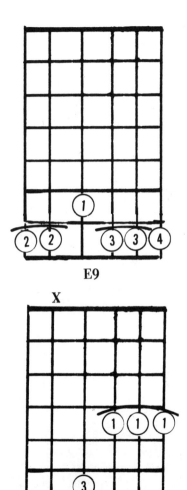

E9

Emaj7

Em

Em7

Em7

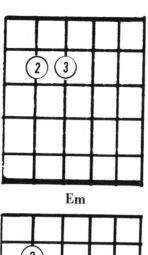

Em

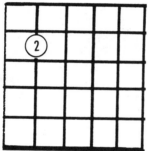

Em7

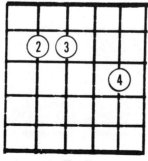

Em7

Em9

Em

Em

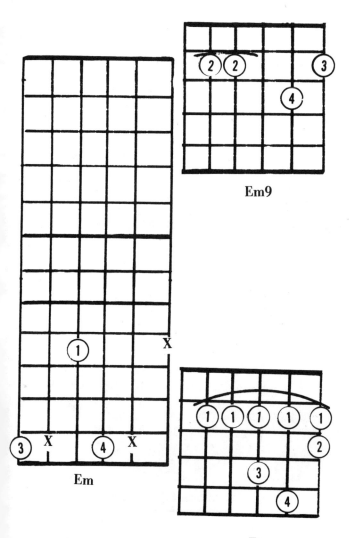

Em9

Em

Em

Em7

Em

Em (9)

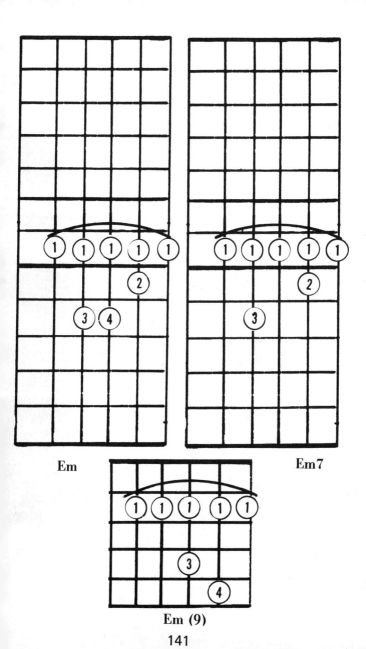

Em

Em7

Em (9)

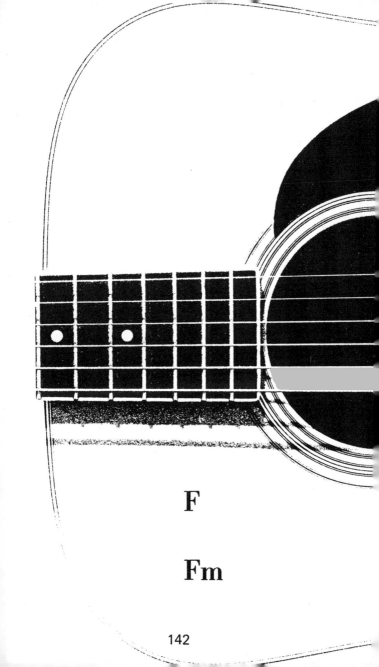

F

Fm

F♯

G♭

F

F7

F7

144

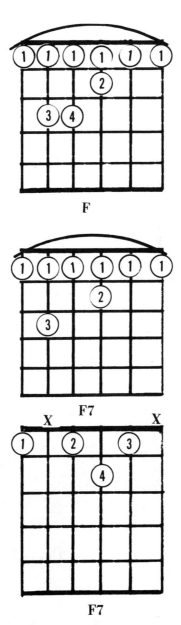

F

F7

F7

F6

Thumb F6

Thumb F

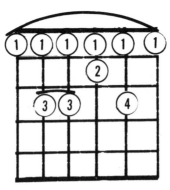

F6

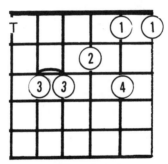

Thumb F6

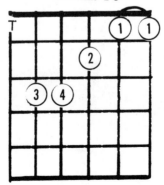

Thumb F

Fmaj7

Fmaj7

F7

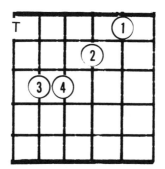

Fmaj7

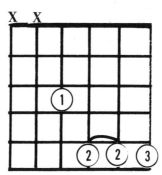

Fmaj7

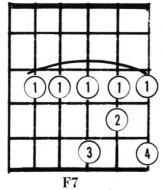

F7

F

F7

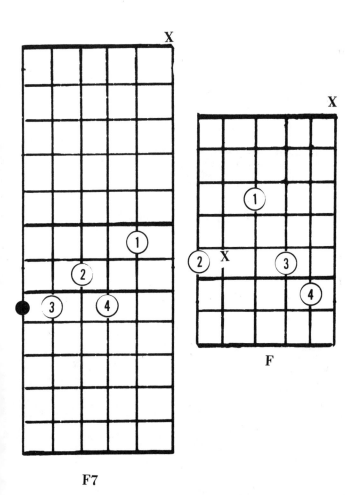

F7

F

F (D-form)

F9

152

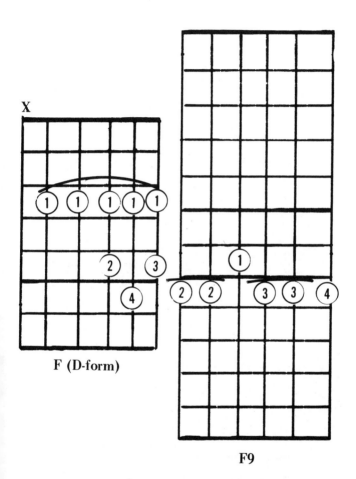

X

F (D-form)

F9

Fm7

Fm

Fm

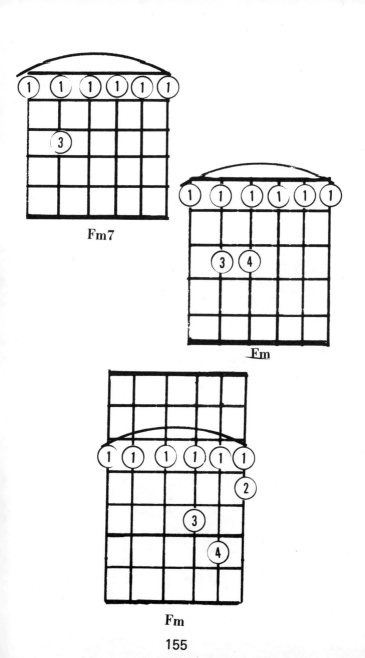

Fm7

Fm

Fm

155

Fm (9)

Thumb Fm

Fm

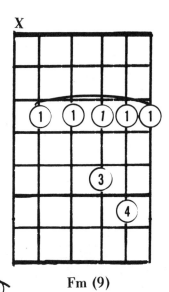

Fm (9)

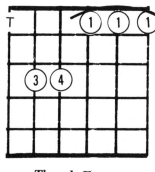

Thumb Fm

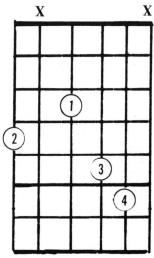

Fm

F♯   G♭

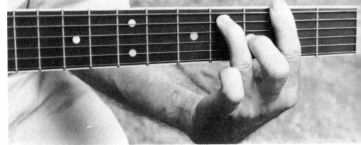

F♯7   G♭7

Thumb F♯   Thumb G♭

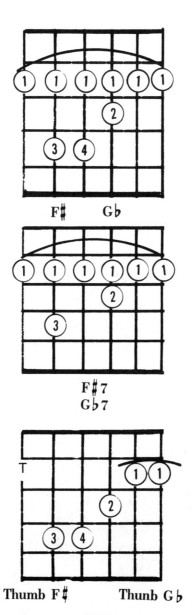

F#   Gb

F#7
Gb7

Thumb F#   Thunb Gb

F♯7   G♭7

F♯maj7   G♭maj7

F♯m   G♭m

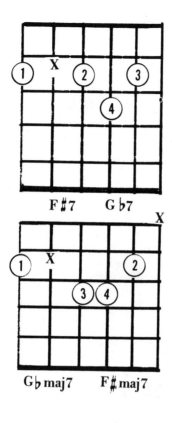

F#7   Gb7

Gb maj7   F#maj7

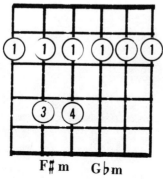

F#m   Gbm

F♯m7   G♭m7

F♯7   G♭7

F♯   G♭

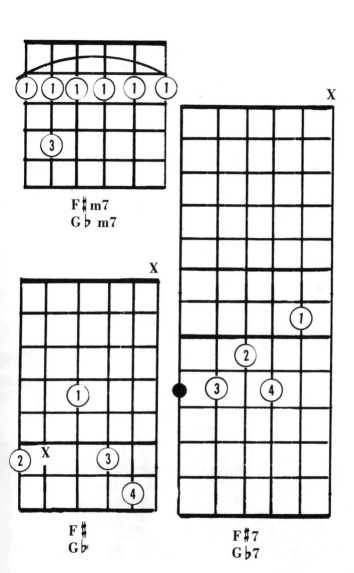

F#m7
Gbm7

F#
Gb

F#7
Gb7

163

PLAY THE GUITAR

GUITAR

GUITAR

G

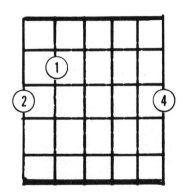

G   G♯

Gm   A♭

G6

G6

G6

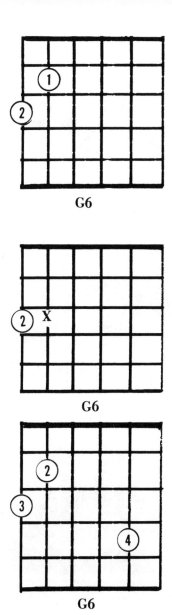

G6

G6

G6

QUICK G/C CHANGES

Church G

Church C

G7

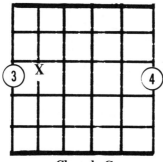

Church G

FOR QUICK G/C CHANGES

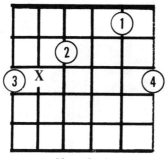

Church C

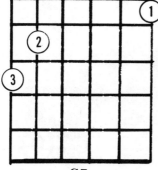

G7

FINGERPICKING   G7

G(9)

G7(6)

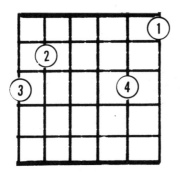

FINGERPICKING
G7

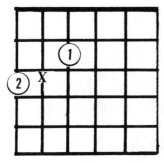

G(9)

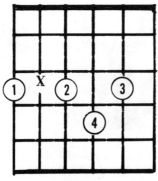

G7(6)

Country G

Bar G

G7

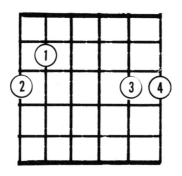

Country G

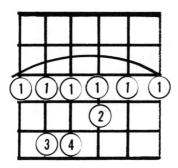

Bar G

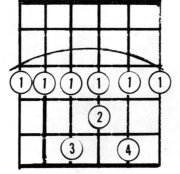

G7

Thumb G

Thumb G6

G6

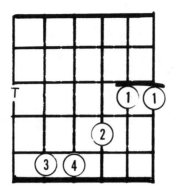

Thumb G

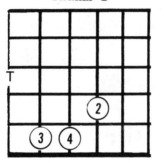

Thumb G6

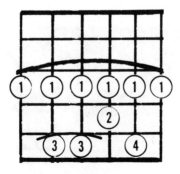

G6

Gdim7

Gdim7

G7

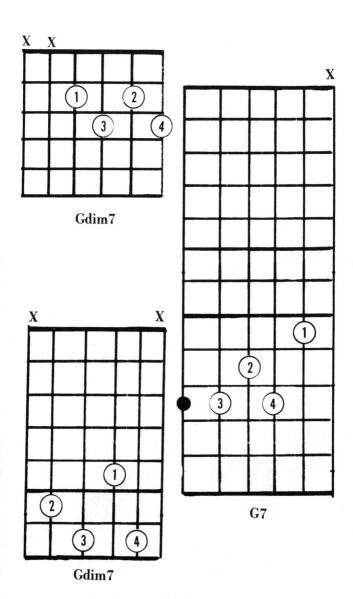

Gdim7

Gdim7

G7

177

Gmaj7

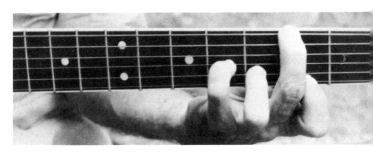

Dumb Gmaj7

Gmaj7

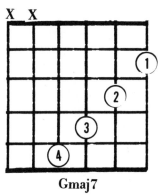

Gmaj7

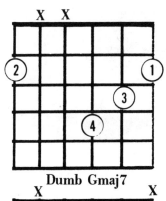

Dumb Gmaj7

Gmaj7

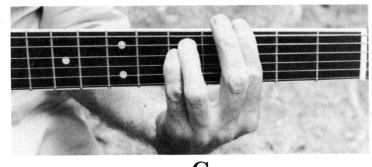

Gm

Gm7

Thumb Gm

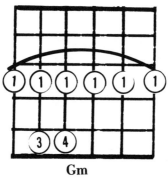

Gm

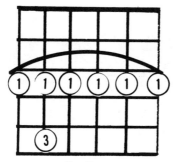

Gm7

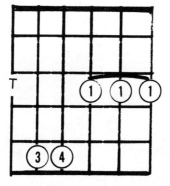

Thumb Gm

Gm

Gm

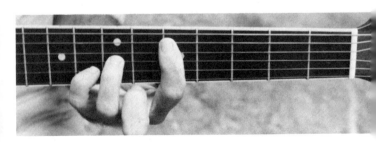

Gm(9)

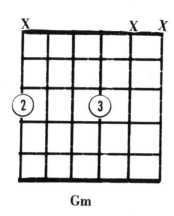

Gm

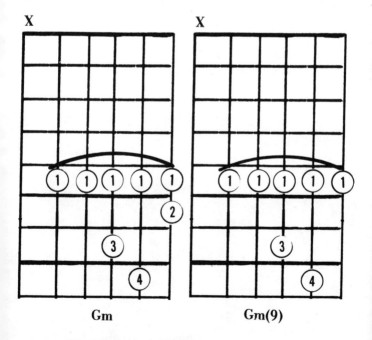

Gm   Gm(9)

G♯7
A♭7

G♯
A♭

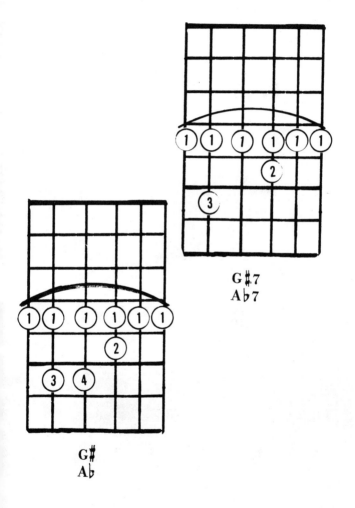

G♯7
A♭7

G♯
A♭

185

G♯maj7   A♭maj7

G♯7   A♭7

G♯   A♭

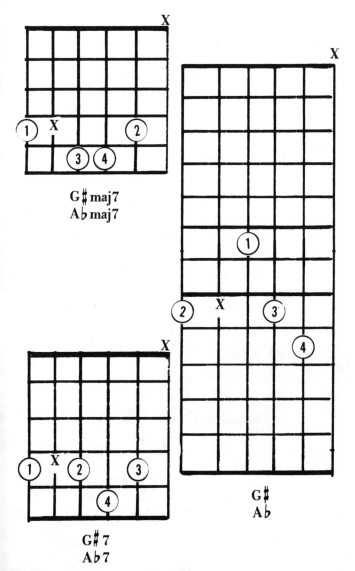

G♯maj7
A♭maj7

G♯7
A♭7

G♯
A♭

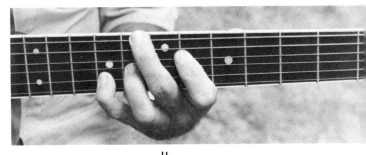

G♯
A♭

G♯ maj7
A♭ maj7

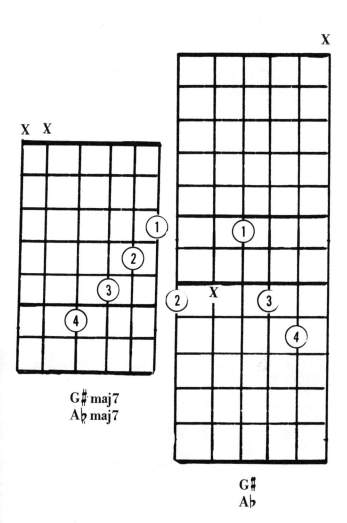

G#maj7
Ab maj7

G#
Ab

189

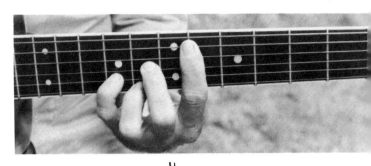

G♯
A♭

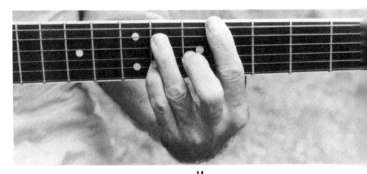

G♯6
A♭6

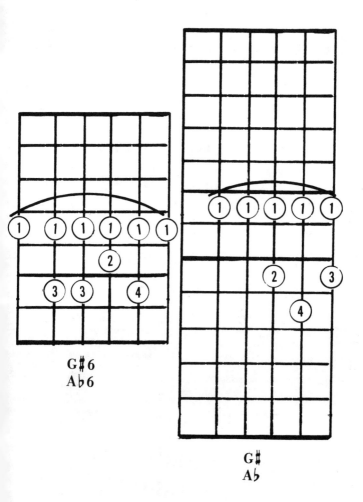

G#6
Ab6

G#
Ab

Thumb G♯
Thumb A♭

Thumb G♯6
Thumb A♭6

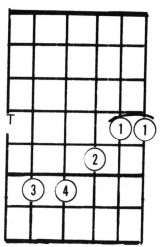

Thumb G♯
Thumb A♭

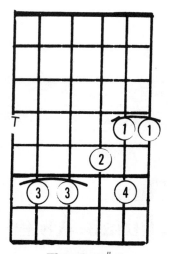

Thumb G♯6
Thumb A♭6

G♯m7
A♭m7

Thumb G♯m7
Thumb A♭m7

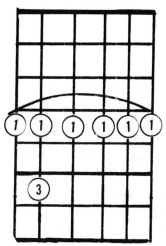

G♯m7
A♭m7

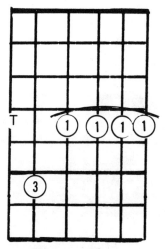

Thumb G♯m7
Thumb A♭m7

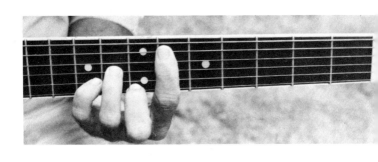

G♯m
A♭m

G♯m
A♭m

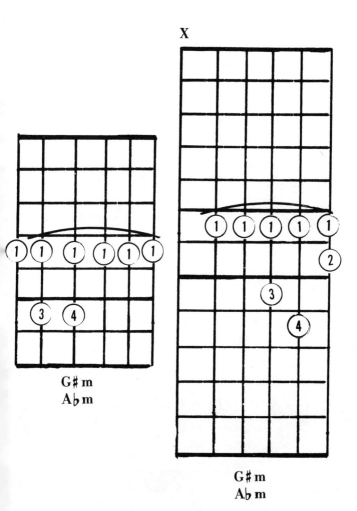

X

G♯m
A♭m

G♯m
A♭m

197

Thumb G#m   A♭m

G#m   A♭m

G#m   A♭m

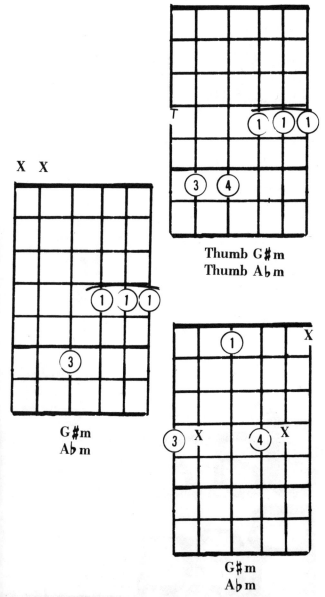

Thumb G♯m
Thumb A♭m

G♯m
A♭m

G♯m
A♭m

199

Blues

Jazz
Rag

Common Blues Chords

3 Note Blues/Jazz Chords

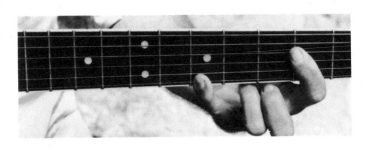

BLUES **A**

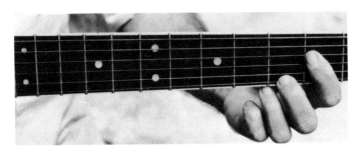

A7

A7

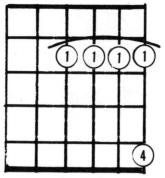

Blues A

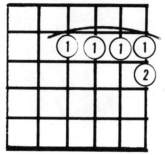

A7

BLUES CHORDS

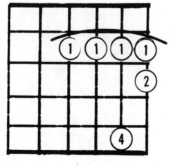

A7

A7

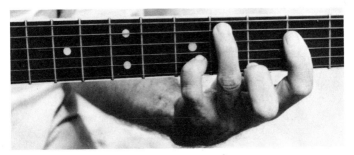

A7

B7 (treble E

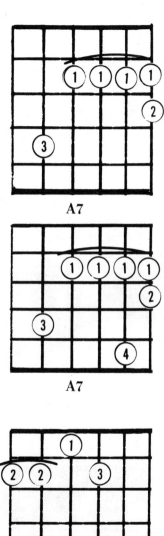

A7

A7

B7 (trebleE

C7

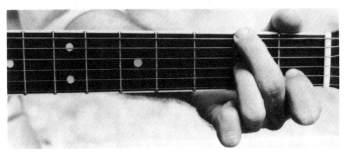

D9

B7

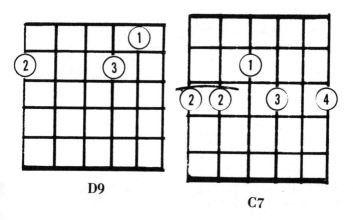

D9

C7

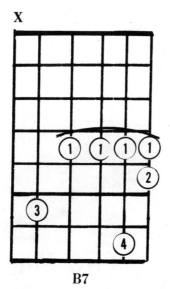

B7

207

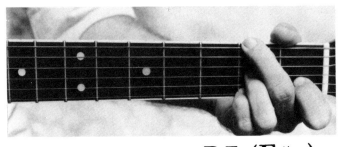

D7 (F#)

D7

Two Finger E

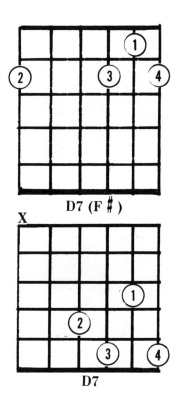

D7 (F♯)

X

D7

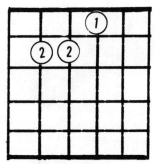

Two Finger E

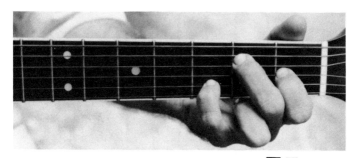

E7

E6

E9

210

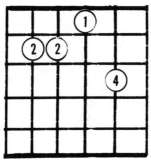

E7

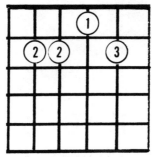

E6

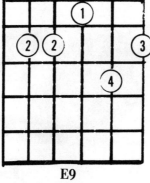

E9

FINGERPICKING E7

FINGERPICKING
Thumb F#7

E7

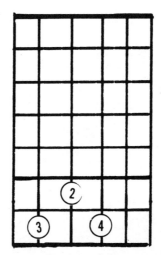

FINGERPICKING E7

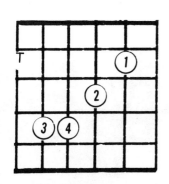

FINGERPICKING
Thumb F♯7

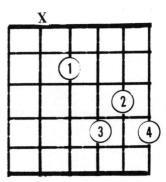

E7

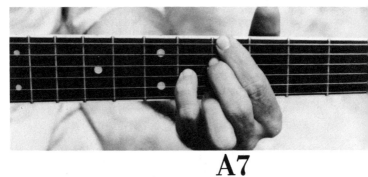

A7

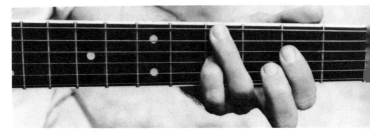

F3

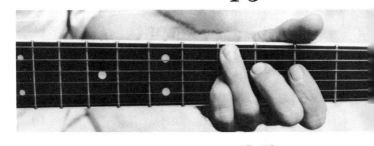

D7

(3 NOTE) BLUES JAZZ CHORDS

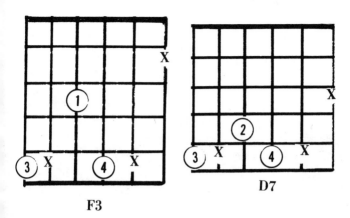

F3

D7

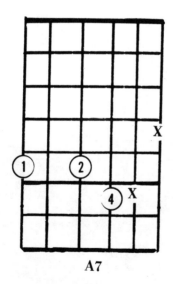

A7

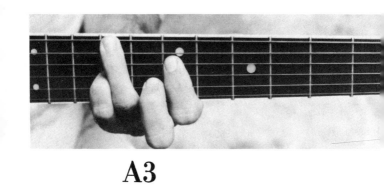

A3

E7

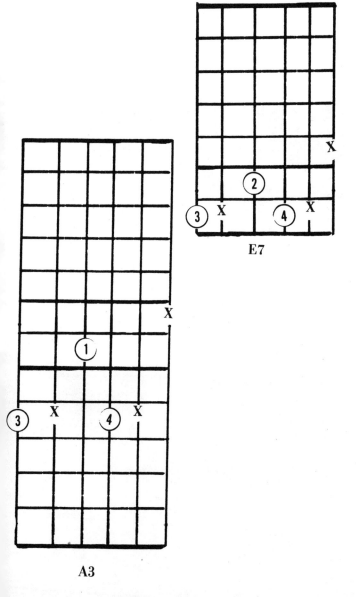

E7

A3

217

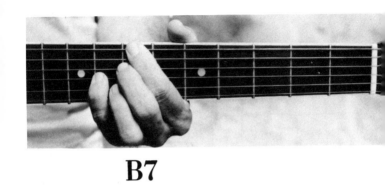

B7

A#7

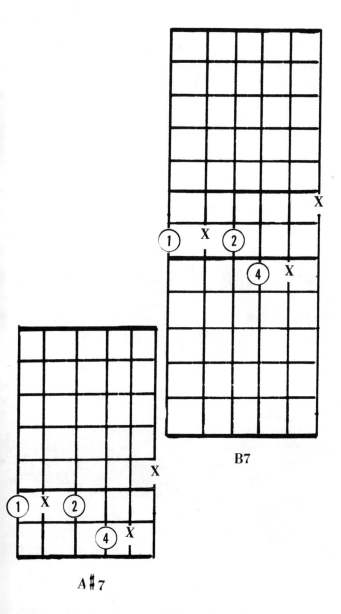

B7

A♯7

219

Am

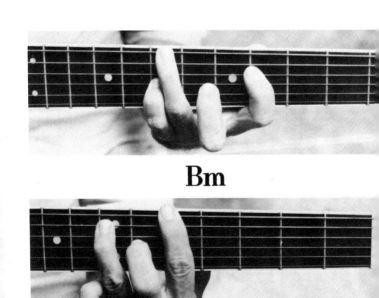

Bm

A

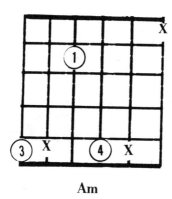

Am

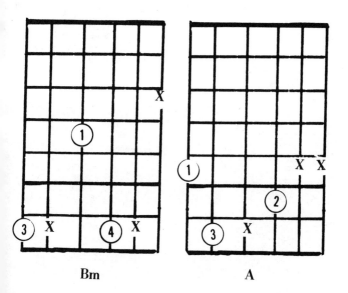

Bm

A

F7

G3

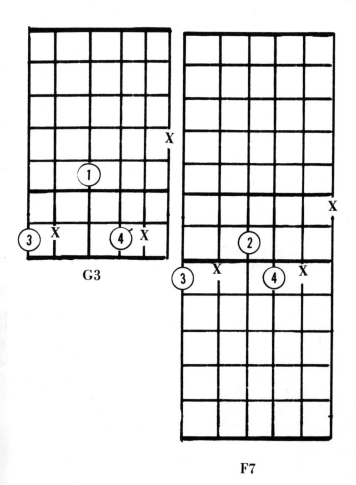

G3

F7